SEASON OF HARVEST

SEASON
OF
HARVEST

Poems by
Linda Blaskey
&
jim bourey

Pond Road Press
Washington, D.C.
North Truro, Mass.

Book design and layout: Patric Pepper

Cover Art: *Black zea* (2004) is by botanical artist Annie Patterson and is used with her permission. The corn was grown by the artist, with seeds provided by Baker Creek Heirloom Seeds, in her garden near London.

Authors' photo: Linda J. Bourey

Additional acknowledgments follow the notes section.

ISBN: 978-1-7336574-1-9

Library of Congress Control Number: 2022932470

Printed in the United States of America.

Pond Road Press
Mary Ann Larkin and Patric Pepper
221 Channing Street NE
Washington, DC 20002
pepperlarkin@juno.com
pondroadpress@hotmail.com

Available through Amazon.com and other online booksellers, and through Pond Road Press.

To our families
whose silent collaboration
behind the scenes
helped make
Season of Harvest
possible

Contents

Preface

One

Two

Three

Preface

In 2013 at an independent bookstore in Dover, Delaware a poetry critique group was developing. The group was a mixed bag of folks, and it was at this meeting that Linda Blaskey and jim bourey first met. It was at this meeting that Linda asked jim if he would send her a few poems to be considered for the *Broadkill Review* where she was the Poetry Editor. He sent the poems and that began a lively correspondence and a strong friendship.

Over the years the two of them talked about a collaborative effort. But Linda was busy writing, fulfilling her editorial duties and contest organizing, and operating her small farm. And jim was busy moving with his wife, also named Linda, to a permanent home on the northern edge of the Adirondack Mountains.

At some point during the recent pandemic, they finally decided that now was the time to work on a collection together. They each chose a dozen poems to exchange and organize into a small manuscript and were pleasantly surprised at how well the poems meshed, how the tones were similar, how the voices were clearly distinct yet complementary. And so, it went forward; more poems, more exchanges of ideas, more doubt, more laughs, until they had what you, dear reader, now have in your hands.

This is a harvesting of work that they have shared with each other, and now are sharing with you. This crop is a representation of two separate views on two very dissimilar lives. The similarity in subject matter was coincidental. But the joy and love they have for their art is what they hope you'll see as you share in their *Season of Harvest*.

For the unlearned, old age is winter; for the learned, it is the season of the harvest.
—Hasidic Saying

How beautifully leaves grow old. How full of light and colour are their last days.
                                                    —John Burroughs

One

By the River

Sit with me in the red chairs that face away from the house.

Watch the brown thrasher in its exposed anxiety.

Breathe deep of the heady mock-orange.

We will not always have this together.

One of us will go before the other.

How different the towhee's *drink your tea!* will sound then.

On the Eve of First Day of Fishing Season 2021

Darkness is waiting in the wings, stage right,
as I face north towards the river. No drama
in the sunset tonight. Nothing more
than an unsettled realization
that something final is on the way ~
sooner than I'd planned. But no one can
truly plan these things. And the river is settling
down now after the roils of winter-melt.

Clarity. Trout shine in pools, caught
by the day's last light, as they hide
from heavy currents. I'm sure I'll rise
early tomorrow, go to that spot
near the bridge, catch a few for breakfast.

To Say the Word Lemon Is to Say
I Won't Argue with You

That is to say I have lived long and learned
when to pucker my mouth shut.
Old aunts and their bridge partners no longer want
to pinch the apples of my cheeks (which, of course,
        is a way to say they are all dead).

It is winter. I pull my sweater tighter,
double the socks on my feet. Do you care
the seat of my pants now sags?

We are bound to each other by years
of milk-meats eaten standing at the kitchen counter,
by the string of evenings with a shared sip of vodka & rocks
& twist of lemon
        (which is to say I don't speak when I drink—
           please refer to the above).

We pat each other in passing, air-kiss at bedtime,
a yank on the blankets and punch to the pillow
then, ah, sweet sleep while the moon's lemon-light
fingers its silent way about the room.

Small Adjustments

I like smoke and lightning,
heavy metal thunder.
　　　　　　—from "Born to Be Wild" by Mars Bonfire

She asked: *Can you describe thunder and lightning in ten words*
　　　　　or less without saying like, or thunder, or lightning,
　　　　　or sound, or flash, or streak, or rumble, or drum?
We were learning about each other at the time.

I failed in my describing, and she wouldn't
forgive that, asked how I could call myself
a writer. She hated the songs I liked,
could not understand my choice of books.

When she wanted to dance, I declined.
When she wanted romance, I offered cheap wine
and cheesesteaks. I marveled as she chose the furniture
for our rooms and the movies we watched
in small theaters. She tolerated my love of hockey,
called it a cute fetish. I let her try out new recipes on me
and didn't complain too much. Eventually

we settled into a life, picked a new genre
of music we could agree on, avoided
discussing storms, traveled tame roads.
Still, I sometimes take my guns to the quarry,
hold one in each hand,
shoot them rapidly
at empty bottles.

Tiny Camp Bakes Her Husband a Pie While He Lives in Sin with Her Sister
(Or So My Grandmother Tells the Tale)

I see her back flexing/relaxing as she rolls the pin over the dough;
the careful squeeze marrying the two crusts together;
the cut-outs shaped like hearts meant to release the build up
of steam during baking.

She walks it up the road—her careful balance of the tin as she goes;
the flour-dusted apron she's forgotten to remove; his ring still on her finger;
the road's chalk rising/gathering around her bare feet and legs.

I wonder why she didn't seek out a bad jar of berries from last year's larder;
stir in some *botulinum,* or a pinch of the poison meant for rats.

Anything but this daily devotion of love.

Imagine Your Parents

imagine your parents
in their marriage bed
or on a cramped back seat
beneath stars or clouds
shedding all or just enough
of their clothing to complete
(are you uncomfortable yet)
that act of love or anger
or indifference that led
to you being here imagining
with reluctance or joy

perhaps such imagining
brings shards of pain
or just embarrassed
warmth at an intimacy
best left in some secret
part of memory's cabinet
somewhere behind your
own first attempts at
love surely much better
than the fumbling that
conjured up your life
and started you

on your own pathway
through the mysteries
of your days always
hoping for just a little
more love and just a little
less sadness

A Chipping Sparrow's Nest

We found it, blown to the ground, on the triangle of grass between
farm gate and fence line.

You wouldn't pick it up even with gloved hands, having grown distant
in this peculiar time of masks and disease.

But I did, this perfect nursery built of horse hair, bird spit, and one bent twig.
Little bird, so much effort made useless.

I think of our children, roosted and gone. Empty nest they call it—
this beauty, this sadness. You touch my face barehanded.

Gardening by Proxy

Four chrysanthemums, medium sized pots, are lined up:
sunrise yellow, rust, some royal robe color I
have no name for, & one green & flowerless.

My garden-tending partner is away. On the phone
she says:

Take that one from the pot,
dig a hole on the east side of the screen house,
plant it, water it.

When will you be home, I ask.

When you need me more than I'm needed here.

Our flowers need you, I say.

They don't count, she answers.

Self-Portrait with Oscillating Fan

Here you sit, window-light with the benevolence
of Vermeer lays across your sweat-slick fingers as they push

the needle through frayed fabric. You try to focus
on the evenness of stitches, the careful in-and-out,

but instead are thinking of that sophomore summer, distracted
each time the fan passes its face by you, its breeze

lifting the hair on your arms like the same occasional breeze
that blew across the cold skin of Haven Lake, how it caressed

your shy exposure, how your tired hand-me-down bathing suit
didn't fit your form, how you worried about shaved legs

and sun-sensitive paleness, how the boys ran by you,
cannonballed into the lake, their heads bobbing back up

slick and wet, faces shining bright as marbles. And you,
gangly, hadn't yet learned to swim.

Apocalyptic Slow Dance 1967

Joplin was screaming
trying to give away pieces
of her heart while
Jenny Chou and I
were off to the side
of the stage
nearly welded, making
small movements
foot and body,

We both should have been
stoned, but I held back
faked deep tokes
planned my escape,
wondered if bass fishing
was in my future and
if this serious woman
had a recipe for the catch.
I noticed
the singer's nipples.

Jenny wasn't kind
but she tolerated
my foolish naïve heart.
Tonight she would
drop me. Thank you
would be my only
words as the dance ended,
as the show ended.

Walking Alone to Hopewell Furnace

Somewhere in the pages of *The Complete Walker*, Colin Fletcher
advises a sturdy walking stick, a good hat, and a roomy pack.

All I carry is the weight of you and what I've left behind.
Are you napping midafternoon? Is the dog in your lap?

I've reached the eastern edge of Hopewell Lake—canoed across
when our boys were young—

and snapped a photo of two people in a boat, drifting.
Not us—just the simple dream of us.

I look back at the distance I've covered; at the small snake
crushed into the gravel; the stump of a tree with its heart dug out.

Autumn Poem 2020

This year's fall is venomous,
spiteful and angry and ailing.

Here on the river, we barely glance
at wicked news,
or check on virus numbers,
or listen to electioneering meanness.

Sorting it all out is not our job.
Leave it to the young and able.
They'll blame us for what's left anyway.
Bitterness goes both ways.

Trees transform, as always.
Temperatures drop a little
each day, though the occasional
sweaty surprise still shows up.

We work on surviving:
stack more firewood,
stock up the larder,
stay away from people we never liked anyway,
do pre-winter chores.

Soon we'll listen to the barren wind,
watch the most fragile beings leave our woods,
call for the snowplow, start the first fire of the season,
                    hope for a kinder spring.

Mimosa

Albizia julibrissin
        —meaning silk tree, meaning tree of sleep

Today they are thought trash trees, invasives.
Yet I am loath to take down the one
whose canopy rises above the barn roof,

casts shade and cool. Honeybees and hummers,
butterflies are drawn to the abundance of summer's blooms.

Grandfather had one—purposefully planted, well maintained.
When he died his house was lifted by strangers
from its foundation, moved. The mimosa left behind.

Did you know these trees are called *shabdkhosh*—
Persian for night sleeper because their leaves curl in
on themselves at the coming of dark. Also when it rains.

Spillage

I haul the fifty-pound bag
of feed, no longer
an easy chore, to the barn.

As I lower it
to the storage bin
it bursts at the seam,

spills tan and brown and gold
in patches of sunlight, a near perfect
circle on rough planks.

First, I curse.
Next the broom
and dustpan.

Sweep and scoop
add to the pigs' trough.
Movements blend—

rounded, arced.
An accident has become
a pleasant routine.

I hear birds at the empty
windows, complaining.

Motel at the Water's Edge

after Jack Gilbert

The ceiling fan turns in lazy rotation.
He is lying on his side, shades drawn.
The party is outside, red lights, white lights
strung from tree to tree; and there is also the laughter.
Someone stumbles against the door
and he remembers the sidewalk,
the trip, how he caught her, kept her
from falling. They had already fallen. He thinks
of her and of all the unfamiliar women since.
The receding tide reveals what lives in mud and brine.

Doing Dishes

By hand, I mean. Standing at the sink,
a hot froth of dishwater in the right section.
My method: silverware and glassware already
submerged, plates and bowls in a stack pre-
rinsed and ready to go in next, pots and pans
piled on the stove waiting their turn. Others
have different systems. I have mine, designed
according to my sense of universal order.

There was a time when I would try
(and fail) to convert Linda to my system.
She has hers, logical as mine, yet different.

Mine allows time for window gazing, for birds
and chipmunks and squirrels. Falling rain, leaves
and snow can slow me down, but I never lose
my sequence, my rhythm. Phillips Brooks said

It is while you are patiently toiling
at the little tasks of life that the meaning
and shape of the great whole of life dawn on you.

I say, *Well, maybe.* Doing dishes never offered up
any great revelation about life. It's just something
that needs to be done. And I prefer Palmolive, not Dawn.

TWO

Prey/Predator

Like a horse, what I have seen from one eye, I haven't from the other.

      Lesson learned, lesson lost.

Able to be snuck up on from the blind spot where the past is hidden.

Depth perception—only by how large the subject grows.

By now I should know to veer left or right the larger the love.

The line of its approach indirect.

Eyes in the front of its head.

What Her Horse Was Thinking

You seem so much lighter
than when last you climbed
on my back. Your bones
are closer.

And you were gone so long.
Will you brush?
That stable man does not care.
He's in a rush, a rush
for everything. And never
a carrot, never an apple.
You have two pockets full.

I can wait. Will we stop
at the brook? A drink,
a splash around, words
and gentle hands.
Stay a while. An apple?

Feeding Horses on a Clear New Year's Day
After Weeks of Steady Rain

I have divvied grain and supplements into feed tubs,
tossed orchard grass to the Oldenburg, alfalfa to the aged Thoroughbred.

Annie, I am told, is still able to care for her horses, saviors
for some of us; their needs.

Once, leaning over a glass counter, Annie and I misread *know your worth*
engraved on a silver bracelet as *know your north,* gentle admonition
to keep a constant bearing.

She has lost numbers and letters. This morning her husband
dialed the phone so she could ask me if she had once been a writer.

Bucket half-filled with beet pulp forgotten in my hand,
I listen as the earth sips away pools of standing water.
It sounds like vespers.

Wood for the Fire

This bole is twice twelve feet
long as it lies. My saw
growls and my first cut will rip
through clean. Then once more,
and once more, till time comes
for the maul; swing and split,
each log piece makes six
for the stove.

But a knot, a twist
in the trunk,
will slow the work
and my back
will bend with pain,
if not now, soon.

The Cat in the Window

Somewhere in his past, before she found him, someone
crushed his tail with a rock, beat it with a shovel,
stomped it into the ground with the heel of a boot

until it withered and fell away—but only the damaged part.
The rest? Luxuriant.

He is stretched along the sill, his abbreviated tail
tapping out a lazy tune.

Today he expects only the sun.

How Did That Damned Jay Die

Today
four blue jays attack
birdseed scattered
around one of their
dead relatives.

Yesterday I watched
fresh sap drip from
a just-pruned branch
hanging over
our family plot.

It fell onto the bare
dirt where we
were burying my brother.

The tree is a sugar maple,
its sap sweet this time of year.
The ants haven't yet noticed
their good fortune.

Vulpecula: Little Fox Constellation

This morning, a crippled fox, by parasite or car impact,
I don't know, pulled its hindquarters to the center
of the east pasture.

I herded the dying creature, with my pickup, out of the field
into its natal forest where it curled under a tree.

It staggered and I could have (or should have?) crushed it
with the truck's tires or beaten it with the flat back of a shovel head,

but elected to leave it to the comfort of familiarity.
I turned the truck and drove away; released
the horses to gallop circles on this ground now changed.

A man I know who farms the next field over, would have cursed
the fox, would have drawn pistol and bullet. But I choose the word
stewardship for what I do. What I have done. (What have I done?)

At the table, the rest of the house sleeping,
I shave off a curl of bitter cheese, eat a cold plum.

Cassiopeia in her chair, doomed for her eternity
to contemplate her mistakes, hovers over the woods.

Deeper still, in space, the small constellation attached
to no myth will pulse briefly tonight with added lumens

though no one will see its effort for over 300 light years
and then only through the mirrored assist of an astronomer's scope.

At a Faded Historical Marker
Due East of Salamanca, N.Y.

We followed Oil Spring Road north
a mile or so, hoping to time-travel
to the seventeenth century
when the Seneca tribe brought blankets
to dip into the spring, sop up the oil
that bubbled to the water's surface
then wring out the cloth, fill pots
with magic and medicine and practicality.

When the Europeans came in 1627
Father De La Roche blessed
the place. It was a curiosity,
too small to be of interest
to merchants or exploiters.

The spring is a reservation now, a park,
a not at all popular tourist attraction.
It is quiet, serene, lonely
no competition for the little casino
just up the road.

Oil no longer rises to the top of the water.
Grasses grow wild. Wind whips
between the east and west
ridges. The spring
doesn't notice the wind.
And it doesn't seem to need the oil.

Polaris

The town where I grew up is tucked in folds of sandstone, shale, and chert,
at the heel of red-dirt hills formed not from tectonic clash but domes

built up from Paleozoic ocean floor, layer upon layer of settling silt
and the dying bodies of crinoids. There are caverns still to be spelunked,

and closed grottos, some small as a child's play house. No fossils to be found
except trilobite and ammonite impressions in sedimentary stone;

artifact arrowheads flint-knapped into shape by Osage and Quapaw.
We lived above the tree line on a bald knob visible from the valley;

people below on the old road looked up at night, strained to see
through car windows the porch light oft mistaken for a steady star

and said *there* as if a benediction bestowed, but it was only our house
of tar paper and tin—hounds in the yard, a flink of cows cud-chewing

in the night, hogs snuffling around the scum-slick pond—but a beacon
to those finding their way while we slept unaware, swimming through

the ancient ocean of our dreams, preserving ourselves for the waking hours.
This is where you capture my hand and I stay, each of us sleeping
serene as stone.

Before the Pardon Came Through

Reentry was along the northern border road.
We reached a fence partially hidden by stones
and new growth maple. We could hear,
far below this sugarbush, the river whispering.
With a sturdy board as a ladder
we scaled the obstruction,
not becoming victims
of spiky barbs. It was night.
We had a candle,
no flashlight. A wavering flame,
our guide. A disquieting thought,
a quote from some long dead poet.
And we entered fresh country,
sneaking back as we had crept away
in those flowery days of the lottery.

My number was ninety-one.
Now, finally, we were splitting up.
She could have stayed behind back then
when we came up to northern Ontario,
avoided three bitter winters
and this shameful walk home.

Jenks Wood Makes His Daily Rounds

each morning, his truck on the skyline road,
      pulling slightly to the left, chert pinging the pan

both hands on the cantankerous wheel, a home-rolled hanging
      from his lip, the *go, Nellie* as they take yet another dusty hill;

a stop at Doshier's, then around the bend to Milligan's,
      and on to Davenport's—milk cans rolled to the road,

kept cold through the night wrapped in wet burlap
      waiting, while cream separates and rich butterfat rises;

at each house the wife watches from a window, curtain
      drawn back with a finger as she tallies in her head

a sack of chicken feed, tub of lard, flour and cornmeal, matches,
      no sugar, no coffee—only one can lifted to the truck bed today.

Phlebotomists, Plumbers, Electricians, Surgeons, Poets and Carpenters

For J.B.

Some blood was pulled from my arm
early today. I watched the puncture,
the quick flow into slim vials, that gentle
tug removing the young technician's needle,
then her skilled handling of gauze and tape.

A few moments of businesslike precision
after an hour of masked waiting.

Later, when the mail came,
I received a small book
of poems written by a plumber.
Light and dark stories about
workdays, about mothers
and fathers doing what they do.

As I read, I thought about graceful hands
doing important things; building
walls and houses, putting up light fixtures,
installing bathtubs,
new hips and repurposed hearts,
and drawing luminous blood
so smoothly on a warm April morning.

A Question of Timing

Mowing the fields there are always small deaths—

grasshoppers clinging to stalks; blue sulphurs perched on tasseled grass;
larvae of the lynx moth feeding on fleabane; toads, some laden with eggs

—the too slow

crushed by the weight of water-ballast tires,
or pulled into the chewing blades of the Bush Hog.

And the deaths avoided—just there
the swirled nest made by doe and fawn both gone by daylight;
the rabbits driven from their hiding ahead of the whirring machine.

Later, walking the field, a severed snake, the cracked carapace of a terrapin;

and here the carcass of a feral kitten snatched up by a hawk but let fall
at my approach—its dying so new the eyes still glisten, jeweled by the sun;

the same sun that dropped its dawn light, honeyed and warm,
through my window as I stretched into the yet unblemished day.

What Doesn't Kill You

There isn't much music in computerized
axial tomography, just the beat of my heart
sounding too loud inside my head. Later
it was magnetic resonance imaging, waves
spinning round, looking for concealed
signs of doom. Hold your breath. Release.
Hold, release. Family history, a warning -
or just memories of loggers and miners?

Finally, a conference with my team.
(Am I the captain of this crew?)
A minor blockage, a kink, an ulcer.
Fifty years back this might have killed me,
they say. But not now. Not yet.
One more day of medicine. Release.
No reason why you can't drive yourself.

Reflection

A net, though we don't know its purpose,
is suspended on four poles mid-river—

I say it looks like a cradle,
she says a vulture's wings, spread.

There are no boats this morning though the water is calm,
sparkling like seltzer under the sun's gaze.

The dock is nearly submerged. She says
tides this high are no longer unusual.

The Chester flows forty-three miles, its course a constant,
unlike my meandering life that has brought me here at this age,

to this place, this rocking hammock, sunglasses to mute the glare.

bourey

Unspoken Litanies

and the Kyrie of a chainsaw drifting down . . .
        —from "Getting the Mail" by Galway Kinnell

Before they took it away, which was before
I drifted away; we would sing *Kyrie eleison*
during that most rhythmic litany in the Ordinary.

And old Father Jake did sound like a chainsaw
as he tonelessly chanted the pleas for mercy, insistent
and demanding, always cutting, always quick.

And I'd sit (or stand—I don't remember the position)
smug, knowing the meaning of the words, which were
a mystery to most in the congregation. It all changed

of course, no more Latin, or in this case Greek. All
through those years of exposure to holiness I went along,
unaware of the hidden horrors. A Catholic boys' boarding

school for Christ's sake and I never heard a whisper
of scandal or shame. Forty years later I hear names
in the news—one upper classman, one teacher—confessed

abusers of young boys. And I think again about the good
fortune of drifting. And in a less serious moment I ask
a friend I knew back then if, perhaps, I just wasn't pretty enough.

Three

Gone

My boys are gone from my house
     and I don't want them back (this has everything to do with love).

My parents are *gone* gone
     and I miss them (which has to do with the order of things).

My husband is here,
     though when interrupted in my reveries I wish him gone

—until a sip of his chicory-brewed coffee served in my favorite cup
     and I want him here (which has to do with both marriage
     and combustion).

The Nesting Instincts of Old Men

When our first daughter was *in utero*
my wife began preparing a nest.
A cradle appeared, then storage
places for tiny garments, shiny toys
on strings over the bed, a changing
table. I was enlisted to paint walls,
put up colorful decorations. Her instincts
included things I didn't understand,
but, instinctively, I went along.

Over fifty years later,
A primal urge is moving me to warmth,
to a corner of a room where my chair
must be placed just so, with my books
near at hand, where a blanket sits
within arm's reach, my slippers
exactly where I need them
when my boots come off, where the light
is perfect and a coaster waits
for my evening beverage. Perhaps
it's an instinctive thing, a craving
for a nesting place, a warm waiting room
before a final cold (but unfelt) sleep
or the brightness of a new beginning.

Loveseat

The view from here is lovely.

Cottonwoods, fully leafed out, dapple
the backs of pale horses grazing the tree line.

And mint, green and strong, pushes through the fence,
its fragrance muscular. Or maybe I just wish it so.

What else do I wish:

for us to sit here yet another fifty-one years;
for the fabric stains and rips we've covered
with temporary cloth to fade and mend.

I wish for the ravens that alight on the compost
to be an army of saffron-bellied robins
that march across our lawn like Krishnas.
Nothing mystic about it—I wish for spring.

What I am trying to say is that your eyes are still so blue.

The Intricacies of Intimacy

It may have been
the way
his forehead
leaned on the ear
of his partner
(such a small gesture)
that helped me
understand
how love can ignore
gender.

Unable to Sleep I Read the *Tao Te Ching*

I put the book down, douse the lamp's light and turn in bed,
kneeing the dog over.

The moon lays its ice across our blankets. You are sound asleep, dreaming,
cat curled against your back.

I have long admired the depth of your slumber and how quickly you fall,
undisturbed by my fidgets and the night's quiet shuffles throughout the house.

The carpenter bee I poisoned today with smothering foam—I see her
hanging dead from her bore hole in the barn door,

her front leg reaching down as if to touch something solid. My needful hand
now reaches for you.

You rouse from that slice of sleep that lives between dreams, change position,
then are gone again.

After Sixty Years of Trying, I Learn That Meditation Requires More than Thinking

> *At sunrise coyotes hunt for grass hideouts.*
> —from "Alone in My Study Near the
> Lake I Read Chu Shu Chen's Alone,"
> by DeWitt Clinton

Last night I fell asleep to the song of coyotes.
They were just over the ridge to the south
at the edge of the old forest, where the moon
was lying in the soft tops of spiky white pines.

If I could dream more creatively those songs would have been translated,
would have revealed secrets, without the help of mushrooms or mescal.

At thirteen I dreamed I heard the voice of God.
He didn't sound like a coyote or any other creature
I knew. In fact, He didn't even whisper. Puberty
does strange things to young boys. I followed the voice.

In my new school, gowned in a cassock, praying
for guidance and a good grade on my math test,
I heard the droning of Father Kenney as he explained
the difference between meditation and contemplation.

My prayers were finally done, and I was ready to consider the rumors
of wolves in the dormitory. Their songs didn't echo in the hallways.

Two teachers left the school. Their leaving was sudden
and silent. My friend Tom wept for days. He testified,
went home to Altoona, never came back. Contemplation
didn't come easy to me. And soon I was fifteen; shallow,

arrogant, full of answers (all wrong) and even in my deepest, most
peaceful silences (so rare) I decided to never again imagine divine voices.

The Salted Barn

It sits above the sea on a shelf eroded by the exigencies of nature;

fingers of high tide fling their saline sparkle

onto boards gray as the staddle stones of the barn's foundation,

gray as a gull's wing, as the flyaway strands of my hair.

    (I tell my sons that I have been recently startled by age; feel perched

    on a precipice, aware of the wash.)

A friend, traveling in Dorset, sent the snapshot.

The barn has history she said, glistens in moonlight.

I hope she put her tongue to it, tasted the story, explored the rough grain.

It leans a little—will fall seaward in time.

bourey

Out-of-Practice Backpacking
at the Beginning of My 74th Year

Between every two pines there is a doorway to a new world.
—John Muir

I was down in Gabriels trespassing
on the perimeter road around
the shut-down grounds of the old prison.

As I searched for the less-beaten path
to the back side of Jones Pond I stopped,
lit up the last of my legal limit,

adjusted the unfamiliar weight
irritating my back. My plan was to find
a faintly remembered Adirondack lean-to,

and there, in silence and solitude,
I'd camp for a few days, scribble
in an uncluttered notebook,
come to terms with the concept
of finality. But first,
as I said,

that path
to the lean-to
needed
to appear.

Memory of When She Was Young

—*after a photo by Peggy Kahan*

Her eyes, like hammered tin,
dive the depths—

the lake was silver (as she recalled),
shadow-rippled
        by beating wings.

Below the surface, the words
        I have been here before.

In front of the moon
        geese teach their young to fly

(though she remembers them as swans).

bourey

When to Stop

you do go on
she said
you blather about any
thing and every
thing until
the reader
wants to light
the page on fire
just so they can
quit reading
and I said
but honey
the pages are already
on fire
that's why they don't
stop reading

I really believed that
a long time
ago

48

Gradient

after Arthur Sze

The desk where I sit faces west.
The sun as it breaches behind me
drops its light on the oak outside my window
(not unlike the goshawk who mantles her kill).

Today feels like a good day,
at least a better day than yesterday—

                one hundred thirteen dead at Kabul airport
                another ventilated child lost
                west coast forests, villages incinerated—

The oak, as it is dressed in light, reminds me
I must teach the lost book of yesterday,
the letter not answered,
the door's broken lock and car's fresh dent

to fly away

Plans

He declined dying, my brother,
after his accident,
planned simple
trips in a new car.
He would go visit
Joe down in Delaware.
Or, maybe first, a ride
through the mountains,
stop at that old cemetery
in Standish, look at the family
stones, say hello
to Aunt Mary.

I'll be okay,
he said.

Positive.

But death
had other plans
and found him
on a bed in a hallway,
alone.

Killing Horses

We choose words more comfortable.

Euthanize. Put down. Put to sleep.

But kill is the word. Single syllabic. Hard.

A slug of phenobarb plunged into the vein nestled in the jugular groove.

Sometimes if they are down when the bolus hits their heart, they stand.

Those magnificent muscles full of memory bring them to their feet.

Then the collapse, the vet saying *stand back, stand back.*

     Kill: Etymology: Old English *cwellan* (to murder, execute).

The vet draws up the syringe, says *it's hard to lose the good ones.*

I stroke the familiar of his chestnut coat, then walk away.

     Abandon: Etymology: Middle English *forleven* (to leave behind).

This is too large a death to witness.

Obligatory Autumn Poem

It's early in the season with a clear & hard
North Country sky broken by fast moving
billows of gray/white. Nature's defoliation
has begun, though not in earnest. Here
on the river I call Mr. Fye for three more cords
of wood, check the oil on the snowblower,
plan a few southern journeys
to avoid deep winter days.

Fewer relatives to visit this year.
I record the losses in our family
Bible, a book with a singular purpose now.
I spend some time trying to remember
how I became keeper of these pages.
Then I close it up, head to the shed
to check on snow shovels and salt.

The Pandemic Keeps Us in Our Cars at the Veterinarian's Until Our Name Is Called

I watch a man walk his dog, a large brown dog, a *thumping* dog my dad would have said. The man is bandy-legged, not tall, ball cap on backwards, tight jeans, sports team sweatshirt with the sleeves cut off. A concession to August and self-adulation. His transportation is a Ford 350 Super Duty, Super Cab, FX4, silver, waxed and clean. The ball mount hangs over the parking space line, a lethal projection for the radiator of the next car to pull into that space.

A crop duster passes overhead, the engine revving and backing off as it dives, rises. I squint my eyes to the sky to see where he is laying down his toxic concoction.

I am here for my old cat's chest x-ray to check the size of her heart, which for me has always been large and loving. But today we search for disease. On NPR, Timothy Snyder is interviewed about his new book, his illness, his choice of surgery in Germany. The woman next to my car is leaning against her fender, intent with her phone. She is tan, a golfer I surmise by her clothes and shoes. She appears patient, but her foot taps the hot asphalt while her Weimaraner hangs out the window, nails tapping on the car's finish.

I put my seat back, vaguely consider writing down the name of Snyder's book, lest later I forget. The cat turns in her carrier. The man with the stud truck continues to walk his intact dog. No one smiles or makes eye contact through their windshields. The door to the building opens, someone leaves, someone enters. Such are our days.

A Detailed Description of an Inconsequential Event

Everybody, soon or late, sits down
to a banquet of consequence.
　　　　　　—R.L. Stevenson

The sterile sameness of the fast-food joint
is interrupted by her entrance. Business
suit black, expensive splash of red scarf
around her neck, sensible shoes, computer
bag wearing a groove in her shoulder.

My table, claimed three hours ago,
holds books, notes, computer, almost empty
pens and breakfast trash. I pretend
to write. My muse is constipated. Now
I'm drinking coffee fortified by shots
from a not quite hidden pint of Jameson.

The woman I'm watching orders:
double cheeseburger plain, coffee black.
Card in/out of the payment machine.
No cash for her two-sixty-nine meal.
She comes to my quiet corner, sits
in the booth closest to me, glances
my way. I lean towards her, hold up

my Irish, nod at her coffee cup. She
doesn't smile but picks up her cup, takes
a long swallow, lifts off the lid, tips it my
way. I fill her cup from my bottle. She swirls
three times, takes another long drink, tips
it my way again. I pour. She swirls, turns
to her burger and eats. I watch. Then
I gather my books, papers, computer
put them in my backpack. She looks over.

Her meal is finished, the lid back on her cup.
I leave. She follows.

Driving with the Radio On

I am in what you used to call the chute, this stretch of flickering
cathedral-canopy road, the point you would phone to say you were almost
home.

Francis Lam is telling me how to braise an ox tail (the best way to cook it)
then how, with my fingers, to pick the pieces of meat off—

like we used to pick the meat off of ribs, off of buffalo wings,
our fingers slick with fat—

before you became a vegetarian, before your work stint in a burn unit
when the smell of broiled steak made you ill, before the year you saved

two baby birds, before the fish in the pond rose to the surface
with their kissing mouths to delight you, before we boiled the meat
from the bones of our marriage.

I am in the chute near the end, and Lam has moved on to gnocchi,
that heavy potato pasta that stays with you.

Getting Churched

I snuck in through the side door,
a skinny, naïve white boy
at St. John Baptist Church
down at the corner
of Carter and Grove.

Ed invited me to hear
him sing, to hear his deep
Brook Benton baritone
solos. He said
watch me make those
holy ladies move.

And he sang,
called out for the Spirit
until folks were on their feet
and hallelujah shouts
rang loud.

I sat in fear,
shackled by lack
of understanding
and unholy repression,
born from my brief lifetime
of Catholic miseducation.
Only WE had the answers,
said our books and bishops;
protestants are in error,
joyful gospel shouting
is far worse.

But as I listened,

a few bricks
from those walls
of arrogant
ignorance
came tumbling down.

A Letter to Cecilia Woloch After Reading
Carpathia for the Second Time

This is to let you know I am in the middle of the pages—
no, I mean to say I am in the middle of my morning bed,
my index finger marking the middle pages.

Since first reading, the trees outside my window are different trees,
especially the oak, which has grown ten feet and put out new leaves
of joyful green.

The words in my eyes are different now; and the dress of blue,
and the bridge. I have lost and lost and lost, trying to hold onto sand

and am glad I am old, glad you have given me this mouth agape,
filled with *sky*, filled with *was*, filled with the letting go
of what must leave.

Duet

a Cento

Today feels like a good day.
Grasses grow wild, wind whips.
We listen as the earth sips away pools of standing water
and spend some time trying to remember.

That tree is a sugar maple.
You say it looks like a cradle, filled
with magic and medicine and practicality.
This is where you capture my hand and I stay.

Though we work on surviving
one of us will go before the other,
and the lark in the throat will bend with pain.

Notes

"The Cat in the Window" is for Joyce Enzor Maust.

"Motel at the Water's Edge" uses a phrase from Jack Gilbert's poem "Homage to Wang Wei."

The title of the poem "Polaris" was suggested by Jane C. Miller.

The lines "and the dress of blue, / and the bridge" refer to the cover art of *Carpathia*.

"Duet," a cento, uses lines from poems that appear in the body of *Season of Harvest*.

Acknowledgments

We are grateful to the following journals in which these poems were first published or are forthcoming.

Broadkill Review: "Imagine Your Parents," "When to Stop"
Gargoyle: "The Salted Barn"
MockingHeart Review: "The Pandemic Keeps Us in Our Cars at the Veterinarian's Until Our Name Is Called"
Mojave River Review: "Motel at the Water's Edge," "Gone" (as "Three Kinds of Gone")
New River Press: "Wood for the Fire"
Olney Magazine: "To Say the Word Lemon Is to Say I Won't Argue with You"
One Art: a journal of poetry: "Vulpecula: Little Fox Constellation," "Killing Horses"
Out & About Magazine: "Feeding Horses on a Clear New Year's Day After Weeks of Steady Rain"
Rye Whiskey Review: "A Detailed Description of an Inconsequential Event"

Linda and jim would, together, like to thank Patric Pepper and Mary Ann Larkin of Pond Road Press for their patience and support in bringing *Season of Harvest* to fruition; and Ginny Jewell of Acorn Books, where it all began.

Thank you to the wonderful poetry communities of Southern Delaware and the St. Lawrence Valley, and all their talented and hardworking members.

Thank you to "The Most Important Poets in My Life." You know who you are.

Linda would like to thank Jane C. Miller for her astute critique and for her generosity.

Thank you to jim bourey, fellow collaborator, whose gregariousness balances my reticence.

And, of course, thank you to Mark for sharing this fifty-plus year journey.

jim would like to extend thanks . . .

To my wife Linda and our daughters Monica and Andrea, along with my widespread extended family members who offer so much support and patient goodwill, I offer much love and thanks.

To my dear friend and collaborator Linda Blaskey, who long ago saw something positive in my work and encouraged, advised, pushed, wheedled and cajoled me into trying to improve what I was making. She pointed me towards the best authors, gave me innumerable lessons in reading and writing, helped me become part of the *Broadkill Review* team and encouraged me to submit, submit, submit. To share the pages of this book with her is an honor and a privilege. Having her as a mentor and friend has been pure joy.

To my friend John Saroyan, MD, a thank you for his kind counsel. To Paul Negri and Wayland Stallard, the other two members of the Unknown Writer's Triumvirate, thanks for sharing tales of experience, good advice and a beer or two. To Everett De Moirer for being a good listener and friend, and because I once promised him a mention in a future book.

LINDA BLASKEY IS THE RECIPIENT OF THREE Fellowship Grants in Literature (poetry), including the Master's for 2022, from Delaware Division of the Arts. She is poetry/interview editor emerita for *Broadkill Review*, and coordinator for the Dogfish Head Poetry Prize. She is editor at *Quartet*, an online poetry journal featuring the work of women over fifty. Her work has been selected for inclusion in *Best New Poets* and for the North Carolina Poetry on the Bus project. She is the author of the chapbook, *Farm* (Bay Oak Publishers), the full-length collection, *White Horses* (Mojave River Press), and co-author of *Walking the Sunken Boards* (Pond Road Press). Blaskey spent her childhood on the plains of Kansas and in the Ozark Mountains of Arkansas. She now lives in Sussex County, Delaware with her husband on a small horse and goat farm.

JIM BOUREY IS AN OLD POET FROM the northern edge of the Adirondack Mountains in New York where he lives with his wife, Linda. His collection *The Distance Between Us* was published by Cold River Press in August 2020. His chapbook, *Silence, Interrupted,* was published in 2015 by The Broadkill River Press. His work has also appeared in *Gargoyle, Broadkill Review, Mojave River Review, Rye Whiskey Review* and many other journals and anthologies in print and online. In 2012 and 2014 he was Runner-up for First Place in the Faulkner-Wisdom Poetry Competition. He can often be found reading aloud in dimly lit rooms.

Colophon

Both the display and body text for *Season of Harvest* are set in Centaur MT Pro. Centaur is a digitized version of Bruce Rogers' famous 1929 typeface, designed after the work of Nicolas Jenson, the 15th century printer and punchcutter. The typography designer Frederic Warde was brought on to Rogers' project to create italics after Ludovico degli Arrighi's 16th century typefaces. Jenson's original typeface predated the use of italics. Centaur was created for the Monotype Corporation, which in turn created this digitized version late in the 20th century. Centaur is known for being light and elegant on the page, and has become popular in fine book printing, among other applications. Fonts.com notes, "Centaur continues to be generally acclaimed as the best revival of Jenson's original design—a true Monotype masterwork." Read more about Centaur's history at https://www.fonts.com/font/monotype/centaur/story.

Ornaments designed by Ana Parracho.

This book was printed in the United States of America by Lightning Source LLC, a business unit of the Ingram Content Group.

Also from Pond Road Press

Messages, by Piotr Gwiazda
Parts & Labor, by Gregory Hischak
Radio in the Basement, by Bernard Jankowski
Familiar at First, Then Strange, by Meredith Holmes
Shubad's Crown, by Meredith Holmes
Blue Morning Light, by David Salner
Human Animal, by Anne Becker
Crooked Speech, by Sid Gold
Tough Heaven: Poems of Pittsburgh, by Jack Gilbert
Walking the Sunken Boards, by Linda Blaskey, Gail Braune Comorat, Wendy Elizabeth Ingersoll and Jane C. Miller

Available online from Amazon.com and other online booksellers, and from Pond Road Press directly.

Email us at
patric.pepper@yahoo.com
pondroadpress@hotmail.com
maryannlarkin2@yahoo.com

www.ingramcontent.com/pod-product-compliance
Lightning Source LLC
Chambersburg PA
CBHW020907100426
42737CB00044B/698